Our Fragile Dreams

Our Fragile Dreams

Selected Poems (2004–2017)

JOHNNY PERREM

Library of Congress Control Number: 2017907891
ISBN: Hardcover   978-1-5434-8559-2
                 Softcover   978-1-5434-8558-5
                 eBook   978-1-5434-8557-8

Print information available on the last page.

Rev. date: 05/24/2017

To order additional copies of this book, contact:
Xlibris
800-056-3182
www.Xlibrispublishing.co.uk
Orders@Xlibrispublishing.co.uk
754887

Contents

Dedicated to my wife Bernadette, my children Nathan and Lucy, My Granddaughters Nessa and Elizabeth,my step children Darragh, Aoife, Sinéad and Órlaith, my parents Guy and Molly, all my siblings both alive and passed

I Miss My Brother

(Guy RIP- '03)

The hole I feel
Is as deep a chasm as I have ever known
Why? Oh! Why?
Why not me?
I was "kind of ready"
Maybe not quite
I long to know
What is out there-he knows
I want to know
I wish I did not
But I do,
I really do
I miss him, the bugger!
He did not ask and I did not ask him
May I go
He just went
And now we are not whole
One missing, maybe more, maybe less
Stop the loss
It does not need to be
Or does it?
I am sad, but not terminal
We have each other
If we want

Nearly Two Years Now

(My Brother Guy)

I wrote of loss
I wrote of pain
I felt the hole
The gaping void
But what of time?
Why should it heal?
An illusion, a dream
The pain returns, just as acute
Off guard, no warning
Did I betray you with dullness?
I hope not
You are my brother
Part of me
Forgive the lapses
I needed a rest
But now searing hot eyes burning
I thought it was ok
We get used to almost anything
But the feel of our hearts
Forever

In Memory of Mollie

(My Mother RIP)

Your love was as enormous as your pains
Your fragility as great as your strength
Your compassion as great as your hurts
Your tenderness as great as your fears
Your giving as great as your needs
Your understanding as great as your confusion
Your forgiveness as great as your heart
Your humility as great as your wondrous spirit
Your greatness as huge as your deprecation
Your beauty as great as your courage
Your loyalty as great as your life
You are my mother forever
I love you

Second Poem to my Father

(Guy RIP)

You loved your wife
An angel
I think you knew
Bright and beautiful
You could tell
You loved not wisely, but too well
Your courage matched her spirit
Your heart matched her love
Your pain matched her heartache
Your sorrow matched her tears
Spoken fractured
Unspoken bound
Your silence matched her cries
Your compassion her love
Tell me who you are
"I think not"!
I cannot tell you
I am dumb
My speech was taken
Long ago
No words
She knows!

Third Poem to my Father

(Leaving home for England)

We stood on the railway platform
A little early for the train arrival
I am going away
Silence screaming
No words to hear
Tell me
Just once
Tell me
The clock is ticking
Running out of time
Tell me
Just once
Tell me
On the boat
Stood on the deck
Until the land was out of sight
Familiar land disappeared for the present
Old feelings abide
Tell me
Just once
Tell me

Fourth Poem to my Father

(Guy died three months after my mother)

My mother's man
Always
My father
Always
Your past
My mysteries
Your present
My doubts
Your future
My loss
Your sacrifice
My life

Your fears
My terror
Your doubts
My unease
Your words
My comfort
Your touch
My yearning
Your love
My life
Your death
My past
Your soul
My salvation

He Aint Heavy He is my Brother

(My brother Guy)

He aint heavy he is my brother
But he was heavy
Dead weight
I helped carry him
It wasn't too far
His last journey
I bid farewell during those lonely yards
No going back
Terminal
I still feel those short yards
A journey of sorts
No turning back
Gone
The prayers helped a bit
But I miss him still

My Birthday

My Birthday today
Came again
Once more
How many times once more?
Glad to be alive
Wasn't always that way
Sixty-five would be good
Just enough
Just enough for my children and family
Just enough for me
Now it is not enough
Things to do
People to know
Children to grow
Me to grow

Forgiveness outstanding
Grandchildren to come
I wonder when
Wisdom to seek
Nuggets of gold
God I know
Not enough
The nature of man
Who am I?
More years needed
How many required?
A legacy to leave
Much to do

Beware of Death

I will not hear:
The dog bark
The baby cry
My children laugh
My heart sing
My heart break
My heart mend
My soul creak
My soul heal
My sisters' sorrow
My brothers' joy
I will not see:
My babies grow
My children learn
My wisdom becomes deeper
My soul reaches my God
My sisters' joy
My brothers' cry
I will not experience:

The wind
The sun
The rain
The light
The dark
I might not feel:
God's love
My heart pound
My feet stamp
My shoulders ache
My childrens' desires
My wife's love
My friends' friendship
My love of self
My love of others
Be careful for what we wish

My Death

My enemy
My friend
My desire
My question
My fear
My need
My hate
My love
My distance
My failure
My craving
My corpse
My end?

Mary Hillary

(My sister Mary RIP '11)

I heard her hope
I heard her fear
I heard her laughter
I felt her steel
I felt her love
I heard her desire
To live
I felt her readiness
I tried to be calm
I shivered inside
I stood in awe
I stood in love
I love her
What an inspirational leader
My sister Mary

Ground Zero

Bright morning
Nothing to fear
God in the heavens
The planes arrive
Bad news!
Earth shattering
Life and lives sucked away
No mercy
Shattering news
Where is the hope?
Impossible
Not meant to be
Another cross
Too big this time
Carry on
Keep hope alive
Bitter taste
Tomorrow will be better
The cross is our hope

Then There Was Five

The numbers grow
A diminishing balance
Time goes faster
It gets lonlier
It feels more scary
Who is next?
Let it be me
A sacred group
Near the angels
First was Patrick
So so long ago
Then it was Molly
Two months later my father
Indecent haste
Guy was next
Unneccesary
Oh! Lord why Mary?
We shrink and shrivel
With each passing

My Wife-Bernadette

(My war is over)

When all I knew was war
War rooted of rejection
Born of doubt
Born of conflict
Born of fear
Born of despair
Rooted in my own inadequacies
Fuelled and fed from my sense of failure
Grounded in my infrequent sense of hopelessness
Then I found you
The clouds evaporated
The sun shone
The horizon was clear
Fewer doubts
Fewer fears

Windows of opportunity
Despite the losses:
Of parents
Of siblings
Of self
A slow journey
Towards peace
In the shadow times
Now I have less to fear
Much to be grateful for

The Ashes of My Soul

I stand here now,
Crestfallen,
In need of renewal,
My soul, as if in ashes
Scattered
Lost
Dishevelled
Insubstantial
I fear the wind
And the breeze
My ashes may not survive
Self belief
Where will I find it?
Am I a miner ?
I fear the deep.
Like the phoenix
Can I rise again?
Reconstructed
Whole.
My soul intact.
My belief restored.
Man of little faith!

Chains of Office

No more planning or plotting
No need for plagiarisms
A breath of fresh air
As I walk into the forest
Smell the surrounding magic
No spells, no voodoo
Just me at long last
With a little wisdom
Hard earned
The battles are over
Now just my own
Courage still required
I take the fight to me
The loss of years
The battle with health
My fight
But no Caesar anymore

Christmas

The deluge of emotions
Perhaps I shall drown
Christmas!
What a time
Memories
Soft and gentle
Salvation
Loss and forgiveness
Where to turn?
The bitter sweet dilemma
The highs
The lows
The spectacular
The refuge of faith and the birth of hope
The rebirth of love
My mother and father
My sister Mary
My brothers Patrick and Guy
What a journey- not half done
What love
What loss
Love is forever

Christmas Eve

Eternal
Fleeting
Painful
Live giving
Magical
The experience of hope
The anticipation of joy
The essence of magic
Nothing ordinary
Makes me cry
The lights
The darkness
Flickering hopes and dreams
The ceasefire
The cessation of reality
The beginning of dreams
There is always tomorrow
Thank God for children

My Children Make Me Feel Old

Daily miracles unseen
I hold you in my arms
Not so heavy.......
The clouds and dust of time passes
I look up
You above me
Standing tall
You smile with wisdom
Where did you get it?
I shiver and tremble
Where did this change occur?
When did it occur?
Master becomes student
Student becomes master
The old feeble
The young strong

Like a terrifying storm
Everything changes
Almost unrecognisable
No one warned me
What difference would it have made?
The past gone
The present here
Where from here?
Eloquence dims
Now I must listen
A hard lesson
Not taught before

My Children

Back then
When you were born
My world spun
It screamed with excitement
It terrified me
I held you close
You grew and grew
The clouds and dust of time passes
I look up
You above me
Standing tall
You smile with wisdom
Your beauty shines
I hope I helped
The strength of youth

I can relax
The roots are deep
The beauty of creation
Can I take some credit ?
Maybe just a little
They are gods
Beautifully formed
The future ensured
No worries
Thank You

My Woman-Bernadette

I awake in the dark morning hours
Her faint smile makes the darkness fade
Pure magic
My heartbeat rises from low to high and beats faster still
Every day,my lunch box is light with food-just right
Laden heavy with tenderness and love
Her devotion
Ill deserved
Like an angel
Forever loving and always beautiful
The magic of her eyes
The warmth of her touch
A magnetic field
Like the tides and the moon
Ebbying and flowing
A treasure found
A jewel
No price, no sale
Invaluable
Precious
Like a diamond
Forever

When I Am Gone

When I am gone
What will you say and feel?
Will I hear it and feel it?
Will I know?
Be quick
Do not wait too long
The body cools
The voices dim
Will you praise me?
Perhaps diminish me?
What about?
Still need your love
Do not forget
If I can..
I will stay close
Mind you
Warm you
Where will I be?
At the window of heaven
A perfect view
Keep an eye on you
Our hearts attached forever

Depression–The Great Divide

A stranger to me
A stranger to you
No definition
No Light
Afraid of the darkness
The anger
The shame
The mystery
The forces of division
No words
Little articulation
Bemusement
Mumblings
Stalling for time
Hoping......
In a turmoil
No light
Just now and then
A whisper
Voice of the unknown

A glimmer
The odd faint smile
The rebirth of hope
Without justification
Just hope
A few words
Little faith
Desperate for charity
A bare connection
A short circuit
Or a new current of life
Always tomorrow
Hang in there
With hope
Without a rope

The Singer

Wish I could sing
Speak the words ok
Sing the words never
But cry my heart out
Back in school
"Sit down and do not sing"!
In the field
I tried
Alone anywhere
Had a go
Failure
Jealous rage
Forgotten by God
When talents were handed out
I was missing
Wait a minute
A crack in the wall
Thats how the light gets in !
(Thanks Leonard)
Began to write........
But no singing
Words ok
Let them flow
But no singing
Thank you God
Not forgotten after all

My Brother Declan (Fr. Len O.P.)

(Declan RIP)

I made you laugh
I dulled your pain
You left us suddenly
I would have done the same
We were brothers
Almost twins
A common link
A DNA match
I knew your world
Your majestic view
Beyond my understanding
Your love of God and truth
Your life of love and giving

Your gift
My deficit
One poem
Never enough
Your miracles
Your magic
Sleep well
Enjoy your well-earned peace
I love you brother
I know God does
Wait for me
God bless you Fr. Len

My Tears

Something I lost
Something I found
Maybe both
Youth has gone forever
Wisdom creeps through the door
I thought my life was over
I was at the window of heaven
Soon to be parted and ready to say goodbye
I found the depth of love and affection
From most of those I have known
I did not expect a harvest
A barn full of love, care and respect
Enough forever
I do not remember the sowing
Just the harvest
Like a flood of rich ripe corn
It filled my heart and soul to the brim
I am at a crossroads
To those I did not join
Forgive me
To those I cling to
I love you

Time Out-Approaching the End

All my yesterdays at an end
A little while of tomorrows remain
Can I stand the white searing heat and pain of goodbyes?
All the loves of my life
Like pillars
Indestructible
But not me
What shall I wear for my journey
A rough uneven fabric of my history
Potted with mediocrity and a few moments of inspiration
I shall retrace my steps and stumbles
I shall seek forgiveness
I shall offer my thanks and gratitude for
all the riches I have been given
The lights will dim
The sounds become more distant
The loves will never dull
The march of time will have it's way
My fate is sealed

The Loves of my Life

(The women I have loved)

Like cement & mortar
Built the foundations and walls of my life
Held me together like bonded glue
In the stormy days and nights
Unpleasant dreams
Their love is like flower petals
Laid on the rocky road of life and pain
Where destiny is unsure
And safety uncertain and disconnected
Cushioned by warmth and heartfelt love
Tender as a warm pillow
How could I be laid low?
The perfumed air of deep connections
Like the finest wines
I resist the unbearable rocky rising road
The loves continue despite so much absence
Better born lucky than rich
These loves allow me to endure
The ravages of disease
The threat of ending
God bless my women forever
Poetry in my heart

A Wonderful Lady of Grace

(In deep gratitude to Professor Karen Redmond
who removed part of my lung in December 2014)

The light of dawn springs forth
Your words touched me
Somewhere deep,
Somewhere tender
You might be cured
"I want you cured"
Magic energy
Mystical hope
Touch of genius
Laced with a "special" love
Of caring and deep compassion
Desire to heal
Desire to be healed
Not earned
Freely given
To pass onto my loved ones
Gift of life
Gift of love
Thanks Karen

The Silence

The bells have dulled to silent
The Reaper is on vacation
I wonder how long he will be?
In no rush I hope!
Make hay while the sun shines
Even on a cloudy day
The light of hope
The light of life
The chance to reach out
To connect
The marching bands have retired
For now at least!
I wonder how long they will be?
In no rush I hope!
Go gently and live well
I wonder how long I will be?
Sow well
Enjoy the harvests
How many I cannot know
Treasure them
It's not infinite

Our Fragile Dreams

I will take the thread that connects us
And weave it into a soft garment
With pockets inside and out
To hold our spirits and souls
Our celibate and other desires
Our spoken and unspoken thoughts
Before they evaporate
A mystical fabric to lie on
To rest and find ourselves
To discover and share the secrets of our lives
A unique journey
To find the expressions and voice that need to surface
Before it's too late
Most of our lives behind us
Doors we never opened
Find the keys together
Walk on the sacred ground
Of our unspoken and yet unfulfilled dreams

My Poetry

They are my words
My meaning and my intent
Not always sure exactly what they mean
It sort of changes!
A connection from my heart and soul to yours
I hope!
A signal output to humanity
A noisy signal at times
Sometimes the connection succeeds
Sometimes not so sure
My heart and soul is my currency
I do not know how it trades
It is all I have to offer
Maybe a little wisdom
Enough years under my belt
Scars to prove it
Scars to disprove it
My desire to reach out to you
To change
Perhaps

And What of My Ashes

I lived and I will die
I was loved
No chains strong enough
To hold me here
Where shall I go?
The tides of the eternal earth are forever
Bury me or burn me
I prefer the longer process!
Time to be purified
To reflect
Time to be forgiven
To regret the mistakes
The miscalculations
A few victories to savour
Like precious jewels
Got me across the line
To be saved

Music- Poetry of Our Lives

I hear the chords
I cannot play
They penetrate my soul
Like a force of nature fill my heart
Inspire and crush my soul
Sometimes the music submerges me like a torrent river
With tears and destruction
With love and tenderness
With moving and painful memories
I weep in private to hide my pain
Grateful for the present, forgotten and distant memories
Don't forget the memories
Remember who I was
Who I still am
We are aged with time
But not always so much in our spirit and soul
Forget nothing
The past is worth keeping
Perhaps not so gracious
But still who we are

The Prostate

Just one
Not so big, not so small
About the size of a walnut
Familiarity breeds contempt
It does what it does
Connected to so many nerves
No problem
Until it gets on my nerves
The big C
What to do?
Choices to make
Hormones?
Radiation?
Surgery?
If I have the nerve!
Take it out
Safer
The loss
The impact
Me

Who I am and what I can and will deliver
One of the motorways of my communication
Gone
I will still live
My heart burns bright
Love has different forms and avenues
Regrets?
Some

The Fruit Tree

It blossoms
It grows
It is beautiful
Needs very little help from us
It bears fruit
Sweet and life giving
But then the season ends
And departs
The loss of life as we see it
The courage to believe
It will not leave us
Different eyes required
It will reconnect with us
It will return

I Worked for Forty-Seven Years

So long

Yet so quick

I did not know

How old I would be at the finish

Somewhat depleted

Sometimes I yearned for the end date

Mostly I feared it

The need to be someone

The fear of being no one

Uncertain outcomes

Closer to the end than the beginning

The foggy days

Hid the truth

As to the speed and direction of the journey

Assisted by unexpected illnesses

Dulled the senses for a while

Clarified my perspective

So here I am

Forty-seven years have past

The gains and the losses

Time for another few rounds

A few lessons learned

Some missed

I wonder if it sounds familiar

To Fill the Shoes of my Father

I can only estimate the size
Imagine the fit
A mismatch
So much for DNA
His proud life and history
Versus my mediocrity
I did not represent my country
I did not speak eloquently about history and life
But I did find my voice and passions
To express my feelings and heart
I laughed and I hugged
I cried and wiped away mine and others' tears
I led men and tried to inspire
Fill them with dignity and purpose
I did not retreat
I sought answers
Still do
He had a bigger shadow somehow
Maybe I stopped growing
Hey! he is my father

What Just Might Have Been

(About my first love)

Today no tears
No real sorrows
Just a tinge of regret
Back then a most beautiful world of glorious possibility
A goddess before me
That is what I saw
I was walking on sacred ground
Almost afraid to breathe
A world of dreams being realized
No fears except for a sense of inadequacy
A fear that I might fail
Just not be enough
Unable to deliver what I believed was expected of me
Without the wisdom or experience to know
A fervent prayer to the Almighty
And He replied to me in full
I got my answer!

Wished it could have lasted much longer
It ended on a summer's day
Cycling home
On a lonely country road
My heart broken
As shattered glass in so many bits
But now almost mended
The wisdom of long years
A heavy price
But a great healer
I will be forever grateful

The Hunter

I will pursue my demons
I will expose, squash and destroy
Arrive in the land of the free
All chains broken
The past is not my destiny
The future to be shaped
I will change the course of my history
I will not bow
To the shadows
Or some of the legacies of my past
Find new hope
The reality of human beauty
Must be realised
Felt and expressed
My destiny for so long unknown
Will be fulfilled
A gift for all my children
No tears demanded
Nor provided
My free soul
Will be available
The hunter will have its way
Light the unsure road

2016-One Hundred Years On

We celebrate this century of time
We worship the heroes, the deeds and the dead
That is good
But the vote of the 26th of February 2016 now haunts us
The new "heroes" will all no doubt "die" for their country
But how many will declare life for us all?
The walls will stand
Reconstructed, fortified and decorated
Their existence denied
Except in rhetoric
But the prose since the vote of the 26th
is pure frustration and futility
It engenders desolation, despair and little hope
The egos must have their day
The actors, the stage with words in no short supply
The poetry will persist for a while
Prose will return
Time is not on our side
Generosity is required

Actually it is demanded by those of us who
cared enough to vote on that fateful day
Reforms and change
What wonderful and exciting ideas
Reality is another matter
The votes were born from the painful
experience of our recent past
Did we inherit our former heroes' vision, values and courage
Or do we persist with our petty vanities and words
Time to be mature and equally brave
Will we honour our past century
Or not

A Quiet Angel

(My wife Bernadette)

Sometimes not so quiet
A fierce energy
The heart of a lion
The eyes of a tiger
Especially in foggy mists and times
An anchor in stormy waters
A fire in the depth of winter
A glorious smile in Spring
Forever sowing
Renewing my spirit
My lack of faith
Unable to see
A wisdom beyond words
Catching me out
My blind stupidity
A great treasure
Utterly unrivalled
I am blessed

Nathan

(My son dob:04-11-'82)

Impressive
Tall and handsome
Much bigger than me
Where did this giant of a man come from?
I pinch myself
A sigh of relief
He is mine
How lucky I am
We have our differences one or two
I am the clown of sorts
He admires and appreciates classic history
Sometimes I am the author of jokes

The odd poem
Our Nathan is very bright
A rising, shining star
A man of principle
As I learnt so long ago
Integrity personified
I am compelled to remind myself
To come out of the shadows
Proudly own my responsibility for his being
I cannot wait for the next generation
If time is on my side
My pride will explode
I love my son

We Grow Up and Shed Our Dreams

I had dreams
For quite a while
Beautiful dreams
Uncomplicated and reassuring
Unrealistic without knowing it
Maybe knowing is growing old
Accepting the boundaries and impossibilities
Like changing our skin
Exchanging our soul
Shedding the old
Accepting the new
As a new cloth
Our fading innocence
And true desires

We can learn or not
The art of the possible
The impossibility of life
What was wrong about those dreams
Did not have the wisdom to see
With time our eyes grow dim
The cataracts of our soul
Eventually our heart tries to catch up with our shadows
Thank God for the lag phase
That glimmer of hope
Fading but not extinguished
Until our final act
Dying and praying for understanding
Of our dreams

My First Granddaughter

(Nessa Catherine Perrem-dob:16-04-16)

Born today
16.30 hours local time
5 lbs. and 7 ozs.
New York City
A wondrous day
A glorious result
The magical beginning of a life's journey
The first harvest of a loving sowing
No day from this day
Will ever be the same again
For any of us
I have inherited such riches

And not a little joy
To be savoured and allowed a big smile
A mine has been uncovered
Full of riches and possibilities
A new journey
Both together and separate
Like the reeds in a river bed
My gratitude for this day has no limits
Such endless possibilities of life, joy and growth
I graduated today
A grampa!
My legacy ensured
My love forever
And beyond

I was Abandoned by Me

Years of self-doubt
Grew like an acorn
The struggle for independence and self-belief
The hope of respect and belonging
Living in a desert
Little water for growth and thirst
Not much warmth or hope at night
The inevitable conclusion
The ultimate starvation
I lacked the currency
I could not back myself
Except in stubborn defiance
It was all I knew
The pain of isolation grows
Visits in the darkness
A convincing tale
With a frequency of repetition
My boat was sinking
Time to abandon the lost cause of self
Seek a different journey
Like nature needs adaptation
Find another expression of self
A resurrection
The light of hope and dawn
I live with some joy
A new belief

How I Prepare for My Death

The clouds gather
The medics nod
The spectre of diminishing days
Sunrises and sunsets
The image of saying goodbye
To my children, wife, siblings
And a few friends
Some past loves
I lived with control
Or so I thought
Not now
Wisdom ebbs and flows
Like an aging battery
The inevitable trajectory
Downwards to the end
The original hopes, dreams and crazy optimisms
Fading like a chemical titration to the end point
A familiar sense
A lonely feeling of fading light
The reducing sphere of influence
The ultimate end

Lucy

*(My daughter dob:16-07-'84,
this was written while Lucy was giving birth to Elizabeth)*

My racing heart
The strings so taut
I can think of nothing else
At these moments
Secure and utterly delighted to have
Neasa Catherine amongst us
Hail and hearty
I pray to God for the same outcome again
He spared me for these two precious moments
To witness the miracles
So I should relax a little
The cycle of life
That Monday morning when my beautiful Lucy was born
And so quickly!
Always in a rush like her daddy
Now it is her turn, a lifetime later
To bring another girl to us all
I love Lucy so much

Elizabeth Lucy

*(Waiting for my second grandchild during
her childbirth on 30-05-'16)*

I sit here in awe and terror
You are on your journey to us
Your unique passage
The door has yet to open
You are behind it
My beautiful grandchild
So full of expectation
You will come through
Wobbly and unaware
But just for a while
The almost infinite potential
Embodied in your sweet heart
Full of grace and beauty

Your first smile
Unique and precious
I cannot wait
Your first look
I will melt as ice
Your first word
Will overwhelm me!
Now two priceless gifts of life
Irreplacable
My life is at last full of joy
Without qualification
Welcome Elizabeth Lucy

I Used to Be

I used to be
The knight
With few limitations
That is how it felt
My soul filled with love, courage
And gracious strength
Alas, those days are fading
As the seasons
Except love
Not escaped entirely
Now I feed on the menu of fading strengths
The dreams of yesterdays
The faint hopes for tomorrow
Definite loves of today
Wife, children, granddaughters, siblings
And a few friends
All of them so close
The light of my hopes and dreams
My future
My legacy
My enduring love

The Ambivalence of me

I love you
Always did
I am happy with us
Most times
There are the other times
Bridges and canyons
Deep and wide
No pre calculations or conclusions
The presumptions and assumptions
Taken as read
And a given
Not so,
So not so

The awful sense of reductionism
The impossibility of that impossible process
I am not a vegetable
I will not be reduced
Or indeed condensed
I have wings
They will not be clipped
I will fly until I drop
Not a moment before
Simple defiance
Do not presume on my demise
My spirit lives
My soul is full
For now, at least

Aoife

(My eldest step daughter on her wedding day)

A dream come true
Apparition or miracle
An indisputable energy
Like a bright star
Shining a wonderful light
Amongst us
To brighten up our lives with her beauty
A star over time moving closer
We are dazzled
Actually overcome by her brilliance
It is not constant
It grows and we are in awe!

She moves between us
Glides like a shadow
With a beautiful force
Like an incredible dream
Moves up the isle this one time
An angel of beauty I am certain
A gift to us all
Quite unique
Especially to Ken
And to us all
Such growth across the brief years
A force of nature at its very best
Forever to be treasured and enjoyed
We can be so grateful for the riches and gifts
Of our Aoife

Derick

(My best friend)

He is smarter than me
I would trust him with my life
We pretend to be tough with each other
We never, almost never express affection
Just every so often......
Usually after copious amounts of beverage
The term "buddy" might be used
Each committed to deliver the other's eulogy
God help one of us!
Over forty years of connection
Fraught with peaks and troughs
Never separation
A kiss will never happen
By mutual latent consent.
A horrific thought!
Who will deliver the eulogy?
Who will hear the pearls?
Not me

I Cannot Change the Death Toll of My Legacy

My crippled Father
A hero for the most part
A damaged silent witness for a fair bit
Who are you my father?
No answer
That was the answer!
The void created
No history bequeathed
Except for a void
Just a sparse narrative
Creating a black hole of emptiness
A mystery unresolved
Far beyond our collective graves
Anger and compassion
Strange companions
If it were an election
It would be a very tight finish
Not enough to govern our direction
Bit more than enough to deposit doubt
He did not teach me chess of the heart or soul
But I still love my father

In Honour of Our Mary—Five Years On

(My sister Mary Hillary)

I do not know where to begin
The constant passage of time
Too fast to recollect
Too slow to forget
Like the ship
The Queen Mary
An enormous power
Direction and grace
Leaving a massive churn in its wake
For us all to see, feel and admire
And never forget
Like a cathedral
Filled with history, glory, faith and hope
Irreplaceable
A beacon for us all
Like the lighthouse
Shining such a light to bring us home
She has showed us the way and lit the path
Maybe we can follow
Certainly never forget
I love you Mary

My Brother Michael

An enigma
Not to be explained
But to be understood
Like a deep well
Full of years
Saturated with wisdom
Full of ideas
Deeply mined
Like gold
Just like his heart
We had years of void and distance
Very empty and barren
Now I am enriched
With his charm and wit
His wonderful family and beautiful grandchildren
He is a humble man
Totally unwarranted
Wise and gentle
I love my brother Michael

To The Women I Have Known

Their spirits
Walk along beside me in silence
I hear the rustling leaves
Maybe their energy dissipates nature's golden relics
As my inheritance
A communication of a kind
Constant as the seasons
Especially Autumn
All those goodbyes and mostly gentle partings
Leaves their indelible mark on my soul
Forever
Waiting for some resurrection
That will reawaken my senses

When I Finally Let Go

I drive toward the edge
I always did
I do not know how far away is this edge
All I know is that dusk is approaching
But it will not dim the light of my positivity
But...
The distance shortens
Not the light
The time lessens
Where now is my wisdom?
Not so clear
Actually confused
I am grabbing the branches of my youth and past
Hanging on
My grip weakens
That is how it feels
I do not want to depart from the hazel nut tree
So much part of my childhood
If I fall to the ground
From this majestic and honorable tree
How will life be after the fall

Axel Foley

(Anthony Foley-rugby international and Munster's coach. Died suddenly in October '16.)

Axel, where have you gone?
Your place with us was immense
Still is
Absent without leave
Offside
Our penalty and our price to pay
You left your position on the field of life
A gaping hole in fact
Bigger than that
Our defenses weakened
Perhaps not critically
Our attack without its thrust for now
Our faith in life jarred and shaken

Without you
Your sudden departure
Through that great door
We are down a man
A great man
A friend
Irreplacable
Farewell Axel
Rest as you have earned the prize
Our love travels with you
Now and always
Thanks for the memories
Thank you for being you
You were bigger than life itself
Rest in peace

The Disintegration of My Father

He stood above me
He uttered eloquently
"In the words of Napoleon" etc. etc.
He went to school in Paris
Lycee Henri–IV
How fancy
He became schoolboy fencing champion
Returned to Dublin
Founded the first fencing club in Ireland
Fenced for our country
The chains of his past he endured
The limitations of expression of feelings
The curse of inheritance
Visited upon his children
Reserved for his eight sons
I was not left out
I was outside the pale growing up

"The stupid boy'
I reached out in his final years
A mixture of warmth and jokes
Attempted to dispel the reaches of the past
With very limited recognition
"I got your letter" he muttered with reluctance
The limit of his emotions
My letter told him that I loved him
I drove him to the hospital
Three months after my mother's passing
Too many hours sleeping in the couch
I helped him pass water
An awkward intimate moment
A week later I closed his eyes
A chapter closed
It will never be closed

The Storage of Our Memories

We pass from one day to the next
With a clean slate
No history, no baggage, free
One flaw
We have a heart and a soul
Like a battery storing up our memories
Sometimes forgotten
Never lost
It is a special battery
Ignites into life with the whiff of the past
Music, smell or even a casual innocent word
Transports us to another place
A place of lost or found
A broken promise
A broken heart
A shattered dream
Once full of hope and promise
More than a few of such memories
We carry like a suitcase
On our journey
Sometimes light
Often heavy

Thirty Pieces of Silver

I reflect on the enormity of the election result
And the most remarkable and hideous acceptance of Trump
His character never in doubt
Repeatedly validated before us
I am not in possession of the words to describe this brutal citizen
But to wonder what values underpinned this looming tragedy
Like the fire in a furnace
I burn with rage and incredulity
The furnaces in the Rust Belt
Long since quelled
Except for their memories and their steel
The honest labour, like the furnace fires
Ended
The steel has been replaced with silver
Thirty pieces

Retirement

What is it
A game changer
A switch of gear
A badge for endurance
A long race of persistence
A small gong for wisdom
Maybe both
Maybe just lucky
Could be neither
Learning curves spring to mind
The cessation of that Monday feeling
The loss of an adrenaline rush
And the absence of that Friday high
Indeed, a change of identity
Is required
Where will it come from?
Who issues it?
A gift hard won
Or a curse
It is what we make of it
A new season
Not known to me
New skills
Not practiced
But alive to experience it

Veni Vidi Vici

I wish it were true
That lightning would strike three times
Twice at my lung
Once at my prostate
I am on this earth
To tell the tale
My two granddaughters have been in my arms
When I looked out the clinic window
During those very long weeks
The sunsets seemed more prominent
There were days I did not believe
That I would be spared
The safety nets had been removed
The mirror became a hollow reflection
I no longer recognized me
In that cold and badly lit bathroom mirror

In the clinic
The stats are not so pretty
Maybe I will defy them
Maybe not
Ready to keep an upright gate
My head will not bow
Except to the inevitable
Smiling farewells
Perhaps a little humour
I will have to rely on my past
To tell the tale

Christmas-The Annual Ceasefire

Silence fell on our house
Like gentle snow flakes
No shouts or screams
No recriminations or blame
Replaced by wonderful lights and warmth
The pantry
Unusually full
The sideboard heaved with syphons of lemonade
The fires lighting on two floors
The smell of baking and cooking
Filled my nostrils and my heart
Peace on earth and in our home
But it will not last
The bubble will burst
Returning to the conflicts
A staple diet
I cannot wait for Christmas to return

What Would I Miss?

The sunset
The sunrise
The cool breezes
The blue sky
The billions of stars
The ocean waves
Breaking over the rocks and sands
The smell of ground coffee
None of these
Not at all
Notwithstanding their wondrous beauty
They make me smile
But they are not part of my soul
Unlike my loved ones
Whose smiles warm my heart
Whose tears break it
The connections that bind us
Therein lies the loss and pain
From the window of heaven
I shall keep a watching brief
Always

That Night under the Moon

(A girl I loved when I was eighteen)

All those years back then
About forty-eight have gone by
That summer night in Dunmore East under the bright full moon
Never forgotten
My spirit and soul's needs
Were met in glorious wonder
So unexpected
However briefly the time
In the end
Not so long after
I was second best
That's how it felt on that Christmas day
The reconnection came to pass
The moon shone again
Perhaps not so brightly
Now a gentle love lives
Somewhat quietly
I am grateful
No end to the tender feelings
No end to that gentle love

My Bucket List

I am not dying
Not yet for some time
I hope
Been around a bit
Just sixty-six years this week
What to do for whatever time remaining
Many boxes ticked
Ego scratched and tested
Many itches satisfied
Retired supposedly
Desire for power finally evaporated
Recognition, kind of been there
Cancers have dulled some appetites
Awakened others
A new face with my mask removed
As much honesty as I can lift, hold and carry
Bring to me, my family, friends and the curious few
Leave my legacy for those who will follow me
Nessa, Elizabeth and maybe more
My poetry will be my voice
I do not know the bucket size
It's volume or weight

Not the Years, but the Distance We Travel

Space Exploration
Impressive
Cross the voids we fear so much
Relentlessly fighting our demons
And god like beliefs
No retreat despite the doubts
Move through the fog of our uncertainties
Fighting the chains of our past
Locked onto our souls and spirits
Call it out with stubbornness and quiet dignity
Face our future with all its ambiguities
Laced with the wisdom gleaned from our past
Pick up our courage like a light compass
To guide us into the remaining distance of our lives

The Funeral Pyre

To be a Viking
To die after the good fight
Launched on our way to heaven
On a long boat
Before the flaming arrows
Light up our life
Sailing in a kind of glory
Transmitting all that light
Shining on our past and glorious death
Beats burial
Or the furnace

The Last Day I Saw Guy Alive

(My brother)

Nothing unusual
He came to collect the new sails for his beautiful yacht
Left with me by my sister Mary
Just before the Summer of 2003
He arrived at my home
We sat in the fancy drawing room
Whose ambiance filled me with a most vain arrogance
Maybe complacency or worse
I knew his hurt
I could not but see it for years
I could but feel it for just as long
I was too afraid to engage in those messy conversations
I lacked the courage to try
That evening I heard the rustle of the plastic
bag containing the naggin in his pocket
The sound drowned out my sensibilities to my broken brother

His weakness was mine
The mirror of his pain
Blinded me like the bright sun
He went to bed with his crutch that night
Like many times before
I recognize it for myself
I did not detain him too long
It was easier for me
I watched him carefully shuffle to his car
With his sails
Just after breakfast
I knew, but I did not reach out to my brother
Gone forever

Paul Duffy

(My friend-Paul Duffy RIP 20th.April'17)

It grieves me to say goodbye
I knew you in life
Joie de vivre
Your light and love glittered…
Much more than that
You lightened my heart
Reduced my burdens
And made me laugh
Without effort
We talked a lot in those final yards
Toward your journey's end
I feared for your survival
I felt your pain and fear
I have known these

As you know
Just as we often discussed
Like brothers
I wanted to lift your burden
Not mine to lift
One day I will walk your path
No less painful
Or fearful
Farewell
We will meet again
And laugh!

Lightning Source UK Ltd.
Milton Keynes UK
UKOW04f1520200717
305728UK00001B/94/P